The Sevenfold Journey

The Sevenfold Journey

An autobiographical study

Melanie Taylor

Wynstones Press

Published by
Wynstones Press
Stourbridge
England.

www.wynstonespress.com

First edition 2023

Copyright © Melanie Taylor.
All rights reserved. No part of this publication may be either reproduced or stored by any means whatsoever, including electronic systems, without prior written consent of the copyright holder.

The rights of Melanie Taylor to be identified as the author of this work has been asserted by her in accordance with the Design, Copyright and Patents Act 1988.

Cover photo of *The Pepper Pot*, Cornwall by Roger Driscoll.

Printed in UK.

ISBN 9781915416018

Every time a person faces a new and challenging experience, they may feel alone and without a map.

A serious, life-changing illness is one of the most difficult experiences to navigate. Melanie has written a book about such an experience. Her biography and years of working with the insights of Rudolf Steiner, as well as her own work as a counsellor, map this experience. The way she has written about her illness lifts the personal up to the realm of the universal.

This gives her own illness meaning and makes it possible for others to do the same. To share her story makes us see that we are not alone, and we too can endure and find meaning.

Deborah Ravetz.

A real privilege to read, with deep insights and a golden thread to encourage us all.

Ann Addison, child and family counsellor.

This gripping account outlines a deeply moving personal description of how a seemingly tragic and outwardly disabling life event became the catalyst for an inner journey of spiritual awakening. Melanie's story reveals how her power of determination, personal initiative and spiritual commitment became a transformative agent, not only for her own life but also in her quest to inspire others in social renewal through engaging in therapeutic group work.

Dr James Dyson, retired anthroposophic physician, psychosynthesis psychologist, adult educator, and author of Soul Size.

An early reference to catharsis and the life and learning processes

Once more we must think back to the good Aristotle, who was nearer to the old vision than modern man. A whole library has been written about catharsis, by which to describe the underlying purpose of tragedy. Aristotle says: Tragedy is a connected account of occurrences in human life by which feelings of fear and compassion are aroused; but through the arousing of these feelings, and the course they take, the soul is led to purification, to catharsis.

Because the life-processes become soul-processes, the aesthetic experience of a tragedy carries right into the bodily organism those life-processes which normally accompany fear and compassion. Through tragedy these processes are purified and at the same time ensouled. In Aristotle's definition of catharsis, the entire ensouling of the life-processes is embraced. If you read more of his Poetics you will feel in it something like a breath of this deeper understanding of the aesthetic activity of man, gained not through a modern way of knowledge, but from the old traditions of the Mysteries.

Rudolf Steiner, 1916.[1]

Contents

Foreword
by Laura Targett 11

Introduction
Overview 13

Chapter One
Childhood in Cornwall 17

Chapter Two
The Crisis and Mystery of Illness 22
A Life-changing Event 22

Chapter Three
Seven Life and Learning Processes 30
Transpersonal Experience 31
Reframing and Acceptance 32
Life Processes – Learning Processes 34
Analysis through my reflections on the
    Seven Life and Seven Learning Processes 35
  Life / Learning Process One 36
  Life / Learning Process Two 38
  Life / Learning Process Three 39
  Life / Learning Process Four 41
Action 42
  Life / Learning Process Five 46
  Life / Learning Process Six 48
  Life / Learning Process Seven 49
A Pilgrimage 50

Chapter Four

The Spiritual Archetype of the Journey	55
A Significant Tale	59
Seven stages of a journey's archetype	66
First stage	67
Second stage	68
Third stage	69
Fourth stage	70
Fifth stage	72
Sixth stage	73
Seventh stage	74
Further reflections on Building Bridges and the Oasis Project – the catalysts	75
Names and themes of the three Pathways of Oasis, indicating their rites of passage	77
Summary	78
Conclusion	79
References	80
Bibliography	82
About the Author	86

Foreword
by Laura Targett

I'm honoured to be writing this foreword to my mother's book and would like to begin by sharing some moments of my experiences as a child, with my amazing mum, who gave me and my two brothers a beautiful childhood; I can almost smell the aroma of the fresh baked bread she regularly made.

She took us for walks in the magical English woodlands where we lived, finding treasures like acorn cups and beech nuts to make mobiles and hats for fairies, encouraging our emerging curiosity and love for the wild places. She took us birdwatching and we discovered an incredible natural bonsai bank in the neighbouring woodland, full of the smells of wild thyme and marjoram and bonsai spruce, where we used to regularly visit and feast on tiny woodland strawberries, discover rare butterflies and listen to a symphony of birdsong...

She baked with us, painted with us, encouraged our art and craft, sent us to a Steiner school and chucked out the TV – for which I'll ever be grateful! All those hours we spent in imaginative play, reading books, climbing trees, playing music instead. Mum was a dedicated stay at home Mumma, who did 'parenting' as a craft and art. She also found outlets for her own artistry, making and painting beautiful clocks.

She struggled with chronic pain for a long time and was finally diagnosed with a spinal tumour when I was about twelve. The doctors gave her a few weeks to live unless they operated immediately, and then a life expectancy of just a few years which she's now surpassed many times over!

Mum, who is deeply spiritual, prayed and made a deal with God: that if she was allowed to live until her children grew up, she would do whatever she was meant to do in life.

Within days, she had a huge operation where they operated on her whole spine, removed the tumour, repaired the spine as best they could, and she slowly recovered. However, unfortunately because of the operation and some medical negligence in her post op treatment, she lost the use of her legs. She lost the use of her physical legs but found her spiritual legs, she believes.

It was a huge time in her life, and ours too, of major transition and change as she slowly adjusted to life in a wheelchair, and took on life in a new way, ultimately as the person she's meant to be – training as a counsellor, starting groups, following her passion with heart and soul, running healing retreats and setting up a therapeutic centre, being a mover and shaker and beacon of inspiration in her world.

And things play out in unexpected ways. One way I dealt with the challenges that arose during this time in our lives, was by disappearing into a bubble of music and art. I believe this led me to my own transformative journey with music and now, looking back on nearly three decades of being a professional musician, for that too I'm infinitely grateful.

Love you Mum, and so proud of who you are. May this book reach all those who need to be reminded of the hero's journey that we all undertake in our different ways.

Introduction
Overview

Until one is committed, there is hesitancy, the chance to draw back, always ineffectiveness. Concerning all acts of initiative (and creation), there is one elementary truth, the ignorance of which kills countless ideas and splendid plans. That the moment one definitely commits oneself, then Providence moves, too. All sorts of things occur to help one that would never otherwise have occurred. A whole stream of events issue from the decision, raising in one's favour all manner of unforeseen incidents and meetings and material assistance, which no man could have dreamed would have come his way.[2]
William Hutchinson Murray.

Whatever you can do, or dream you can do, begin it. Boldness has genius, power and magic in it. Begin it now.
J. W. von Goethe (1749-1832).

From first thinking about turning my story into a book, my aim has been to describe, in broad brushstrokes, my life journey, thus bringing a kind of perspective to it. In doing so, I hope to awaken awareness of the wise guide who lives within each one of us and who is willing to help, especially when we are struggling with crisis, illness, loss or despair; a guide that can bring us new courage and hope.

In *Chapter One*, I reflect upon my childhood in Cornwall with the wonder and beauty of nature all around me. I connect this biographical experience on the moors with the imagination of a spiritual journey of coming to earth to be born amidst nature. Inner pictures arose in me that have later drawn forth seven contemplations.

Chapter Two is mainly from the standpoint of the middle phase of my life. I have named this period Crisis and the Mystery of Illness. It was both a crisis and a turning point in my biography when I lost the use of my physical legs but regained a spiritual connection to a renewed purpose in life.

In *Chapter Three*, a time of initiative and outer activity comes together with a study of biographical processes. The chapter draws on my thesis for an MSc. in Integrative Therapeutic Counselling in which I consider the Seven Life and Learning Processes – ideas derived from Rudolf Steiner – using the action research methods of Freshwater and Rolf. I investigate the archetypes which shape the course of a life and attempt to find meaning in my own.

During the years 1994 to 2012, I co-founded the Building Bridges support groups, the Oasis Project and the UK-based Oasis Group Facilitators Training. The Elysia Therapy Centre was also co-founded in 2012 as a response to the closure of Park Attwood Clinic in 2009. A unique community of people had come together supporting these initiatives; what was needed was the touch paper. The Centre and its predecessor aimed to bring healing to a wide group of people from all walks of life, within an organisational framework that was alive, like a beating listening heart organ. This heart was to be open and responsive to the environment and its location within the community. Its aim was to listen to the needs of the clients and therapists themselves as co-participants within it and, importantly, it needed an economic system around it that was free to give and receive, just like a charity does. The Therapeutic Centre in Stourbridge has been running successfully and independently as a Community Benefit Society for many years, with a team of multi-disciplinary and anthroposophical therapists providing care for its clients.

Anchoring the Centre within the framework of a threefold social organisation had been the aim and ideal behind its founding impulse. The heart of the therapy centre itself was actively co-carried at management level by a group of individuals who shared their complementary skills, expertise and capacity within the organisation's holistic aims and ideals. It was highly intensive work both personally, interpersonally, and organisationally. I learnt a tremendous amount during this time on many different levels, then suffered another bout of illness, signalling that I needed to step back and create more balance in my own life. This enabled a transition into a different phase of my journey. Hence writing this book has become possible.

My godfather once said to me that, *'no matter how often you slip on a banana skin on the pavement, you get up and start walking all over again… and again… and again. This is what it means to hold a true spiritual picture in your heart, and this is life as we know it, so deal with it as best you can and never give up hope.'*

Chapter Four reflects upon the notion of an inner and outer journey and what I learnt from the tale of the traveller in the Chymical Wedding and includes Seven Contemplations on the spiritual archetype of the journey.

> *Normalising a crisis within the stream of time in which we live, helps to ground that event with our natural common sense. Bringing structure to its message is a creative work and this activity helps to bring form to our understanding of the crisis. Then, in the sense of a written biographical journey, it becomes reparative, meaning that it heals. It also offers the opportunity to stand back and look at one's life from a greater distance, thus bringing perspective. These factors all help us to swim in the unpredictable river of our lives, rather than hesitating uncertainly on the riverbank or falling in and drowning.*

I trust that you, my dear readers, make sense of this journey and draw from it what you will. My aim has been to offer different perspectives on life and that in sharing my story I have brought this journey to life for you.

Chapter One
Childhood in Cornwall

In the beginning, there was Cornwall. A sense of wonder and mystery arose from the land.

It blew in from the sea, across the moors and lay in wait in the honeyed scent of heather and sharp tang of the bracken. It rose from under my feet in the springy star-shaped mosses and comforting smell of peat. The colours moved from morning to dusk in ever-changing moods and veils of light over land and sea and in the swirling mists.

Butterflies flew up in the sun and bird song fluted each day as the larks rose in the morning light and descended at dusk with their cadence to the setting sun. If you looked closely, you could see them high up like tiny, glittering filaments of light. Sometimes a hawk would come and there would be a chase: dipping, diving and swooping so fast you could not see who would grasp the prize or who would win their flight to freedom.

Granite boulders stood about us on the moors like great, grey sentinels describing a past long gone, yet their stories remained. Giants buried beneath the stones whose histories shimmered in the shade and where I would trespass with care. *The Giants of Towednack*, that mysterious book found by my grandmother, provided written proof of their existence. This was the place I felt nurtured, nourished and intrigued from the earliest age. Who had lived here, who had journeyed here and where did they return to?

Our house was named Beagletodn, which meant Shepherd's Hillock in the old Cornish language. It was situated on the outskirts of a village called Towednack. Names which had a mystery and an ancient ring of their own. I was captivated by stories of journeys from my earliest memories. I literally breathed them in from the land. Intoxicated by each day's brightness and lightness, and when the nights drew in, we would be challenged by our father to walk into the darkest parts of the walled garden and confront our own worst enemies, our fears. He was neither threatening nor cajoling, but just invited us to explore the limits of our self-made boundaries as we knew he had done before us and that it was safe enough to do so.

This was the kind of courage I learnt from him, to try and try again, to win through with stubbornness and endurance, to be protected, yet not to try and avoid our fears or pain. To know that an inner courage makes us resilient despite the obstacles, as long as we are in harmony with nature and prepared to strive toward the truth within ourselves and with others. There was my older sister, who from as far back as I could remember would tell me glorious stories after the lights were turned out, until we both fell asleep. Stories of enchantment, of animals and elves and children who could talk with them and go on adventures throughout the land and far across the moors.

In the daytime, we lived out the stories when we were not at school. Our trusty dog Hadrian, a black labrador, would guard us, never letting us out of sight. He was our father's eyes and ears and would be able to inform him if we ever got into trouble on our journeys, which we occasionally did. Later, there were ponies and 'the galloping patch', a straight, wide grassy track. This was a dangerous place because no matter how hard we tried to go slowly they would gallop very fast along this track, heedless to our commands, until they stopped as unexpectedly as they had started. Did some old earth energy unlock fireworks in their hooves? Or was it a distant battle cry or the ring of an unsheathed sword from an ancient past? Whatever the reason, the desire to gallop at full speed overtook them, and we held onto their rugged manes for dear life.

After the rains, we would drink from water that collected in the small pools on the top of the granite boulders, hollowed out by centuries of rain. The order of drinking we took was children first, horses second, dog third, because Hadrian could always find smaller places to lap his fill. How we never got lost is a mystery to me, though I believe we learnt to remember natural landmarks from our long days wandering the moors. Distinctively shaped boulders, small, crooked trees, patches of bracken of a brighter or darker green; the shape of a hill, occasionally, an ancient, ruined house, and always being attentive and wary by marking our return steps visually. We trusted each other to notice the things the other might have missed, and mostly it worked.

Once, we were overtaken by a fog so thick we could not see our way back. We got soaking wet and very cold and jumped off the ponies to lead them more slowly. Taking off our wellies and socks we then filled our boots with dried grass as soft as hay. Our frozen feet warmed up quickly. We felt resourceful and courageous and let Hadrian take the lead with the command to 'go home'. His incredible sense of smell took us back slowly but surely and he looked back from time to time to make sure that we were still following. Our parents were quite worried until we all reappeared, wet and bedraggled but triumphant.

The ponies were our faster legs and we understood that theirs were the longer and stronger. We valued them as companions for their warmth and strength, as comforting to us as animal friends. We could escape from our imaginary enemies in our stories and get home quickly before darkness, and then, alight with enthusiasm, go out each morning to greet the coming day.

We were taught that if we had ponies, we must learn to treat them with as much care and respect as we would hope to be treated ourselves, that we were responsible for their welfare; this was a condition of ownership. If we came back from riding wet, sodden, exhausted and hungry then their needs must come before our own immediate wants. They should be stabled, dried and fed, before we changed and sat down to eat.

This childhood experience provided a lifetime's gratitude to the animals who served us. In many ways we preferred being with our animals rather than playing with other kids who often proved far more unpredictable to deal with and did not share our 'language'. It was a very particular language built around our knowledge of the moors, our stories and the animals' characters themselves.

There was also a place where only I could go because I was so slight as a young child. An underground stream where you could hear water running quietly under the marshy tussocks in the valley. A little bit scary because I didn't know how deep the water was or how far along the little stream ran, but I could lie on top of the mossy tussocks listening to the water gently flowing underneath. To get there you had to walk across great squishy wedges of grass moving up and down like a giant watery mattress, which was impossible for a heavier person.

As a young man, our father had worked in a museum as an entomologist collecting beetles, butterflies and moths, noting their habitats and the plants they fed on. He passed this love on to us. He had huge volumes about the insects and encouraged us as children to learn what we could about their secret lives. I think a lot of his sculptural work was inspired by them as well as the landscape of the moors.

He still had cabinets full of preserved species. We preferred the living realities, however, and a particular adventure would always get us

Chapter One: Childhood in Cornwall

safely out of house duties or homework. We would go 'caterpillar hunting', a legitimate outdoor activity which always got the parental eye of approval. I should add that both our mother and father were artists and art teachers and I now realise what freedom this gave us as children and what a blessing this was.

Coming back from walks laden with jam jars in which our captives were housed, we were encouraged to take note of the plants they ate, learn their shapes, names and the places where these could be found. Caterpillars are artful masters of disguise, but we soon developed an eye for their markings and colours so closely aligned to the colours of leaf or bark.

Soon we were equipped with caterpillar houses, neatly made small wooden boxes with mosquito netting sides for the air to go through. We supplied the caterpillars with fresh leaves to eat. It was always such a mystery and a joy to see a chrysalis forming and then there was the wait for a butterfly or moth to emerge. Carefully we took these newly hatched creatures outside to fly and find the plants and mates of their choice so that later tiny eggs could be laid, and a new cycle begin in the wild.

Chapter Two
The Crisis and Mystery of Illness

The formative forces from my youth in Cornwall were nurturing and nourishing me, building the bodily strength of my heart, limbs and senses. Without these life-giving forces, I would not have had the strength or capacity to immerse myself into what was to come next.

A Life-changing Event

It was April 1993, I had been reading *The Secret Garden* with my children and we had just got to the place where they had taken the 'wheelchair boy' out into the garden, when I had to go, yet again, to the doctor to see if he could find out what the inexplicable pain was being caused by, in my lower back and legs. 'Melanie,' he said, 'Is there something you haven't been telling me?'

If I had not been telling him something was amiss, there was either something wrong with his ears or I was dreaming! However, on this occasion, when I dragged myself into the surgery, I went initially to the 'Well Woman Clinic'. Something made me represent my misery of the past two years of slowly increasing pain in vivid pictures of self-doubt and despair, to the nurse. She had listened intently and walked wordlessly into the doctor's office; suddenly things started happening, phone calls were made to consultants and within twenty-four hours I found myself at the Brook Hospital in London, awaiting further tests.

Two weeks before, the doctor had said: 'Melanie, we can't rule out the possibility that this is psychosomatic.' Oh God, I thought, I'm going mad, if this pain is all in the head, I can never believe in myself again. But this time the doctor listened; maybe it was the way I was beginning to drag my right leg, perhaps it was my pallor.

This was the start of this other journey I had to make through life, and it was 'critical' in more ways than one. At last, I was being heard, I felt such a huge sense of relief that I was being taken seriously at last. Tests revealed that I was suffering from an ependymoma of the spine, a rare type of cancer that had spread half the length of the spinal cord; a tumour was trapped in the sheath surrounding it and slowly suffocating the flow of spinal fluid to the blood vessels and nerves. I was told that without an operation to remove it, I would shortly become paralyzed and worse, I would probably lose my life within a few years.

I remember sitting in the consultant's office with my husband, in a kind of daze, as he told us that they did not know before they operated exactly what kind of tumour it was. If it were benign, they would perform the delicate operation immediately, if it were malignant, they would continue no further and I may, at most, have a few weeks left to live. Shocked, dazed, uncomprehending, I began to laugh at the ridiculousness of it all. My husband sat there and wept. How absurd that life could be taken away from me on a whim. But whose whim? Did I have a choice in the matter? I knew I had to take their prognoses seriously but was unable to fully comprehend the enormity of it all.

I decided to have a conversation with God. God was the creator and if the Creator was listening, I might have the opportunity to do a deal with Him! This is how I put it: 'Dear God, if you let me live long enough to see my children through school and old enough to cope without me as "Mum", I promise I will do the thing that I am most afraid of doing that will be of help to the world.' Well, I knew what that was all right: it was to take up my profession as a teacher! I had trained as a teacher in the early seventies and had, with some relief, found out I was expecting our first child shortly after applying for a job. Marvellous, I thought, I do not have to teach, I can look after the family, make bread, do the gardening and all sorts of 'homey' things.

I woke up from an eight-hour operation on the 19th of May 1993, acutely distressed, my mouth agonizingly dry and unable to speak. I was covered with a silver foil sheet; my hands were on my chest under it and shaking uncontrollably; the sheet rattled and glittered. I looked to the end of the bed and saw a figure dressed in blue, with a blue face mask and cap on his head. He looked into my eyes with an endlessly compassionate, loving gaze, knowing how I felt, his eyes were the deepest, richest brown I had ever seen. He stepped towards me, took both his hands and without a word placed them over my own, on my chest. The rattling stopped, my anxiety vanished and then he stepped back again. This time it was worse, the distress, the pain, the anxiety, the shaking; he came forward again and made the same gesture.

Endless love streamed into me from his gaze once more, with the warm pressure of his hands on mine, stilling all my pain. Unspoken words quite clearly spoke into my consciousness. 'It's going to be alright.' I relaxed, knowing it would be so. For weeks I wondered if I would recognise him without his mask on when they made the rounds in hospital; I looked into all the brown eyes that I could see but could not find his. I was almost glad; I did not know if I would have been able to bear the intensity of the encounter again.

Since then, my time at the Brook was blessed, my recovery went well, the tumour was found to be 'benign-ish', a wonderful 'medical' term that meant I was not going to die in three weeks; but if I had radiotherapy to treat the remaining part of the tumour they had

Chapter Two: The Crisis and Mystery of Illness

not been able to remove, because of its proximity to highly delicate nerves, I may well have ten years or more to live. I had to lie flat for three weeks, turned over every two hours, drink lots of water, pipes and tubes everywhere.

Every afternoon my husband would come up from the school where he taught and sit with me, willing me to get better, supportive and loving. My mother looked after the children, it was so painful for them to see me like this and so terribly painful for me not to be able to care for them. I progressed from wiggling my toes to flexing my feet to standing unassisted and then to shuffling about on a Zimmer frame. Three months later I went home, still dependent on heavy painkillers, incontinent, disorientated, mobile, and with a life expectancy extension clause. I learnt to walk again, but by August had to go into hospital for another operation, to have a hysterectomy, both a blessing and a terrible loss.

Then the consultant said we should start the radiotherapy treatment that autumn. Seriously wondering if this was a good course of action, and deeply afraid of this form of treatment, which had associations for me of wiping out the inhabitants of Hiroshima and Nagasaki through the atom bomb, I was acutely aware I was dicing with one of the most powerful negative energies in the world. Nothing would have induced me to have this treatment had it not been for the carrot of prolonging my life expectancy for my family's sake, which I was advised it would. Three to four years before a re-occurrence without this treatment, ten years or more with it, they said.

I had to call on God again. I decided to say the Lord's Prayer every time I went under the radiotherapy machine, twice: once for the lower spine and once for the upper part, timed precisely to coincide with the treatment, so that at no time was I unprotected and alone with 'it'.

Truthfully, it was the only thing I could do in the circumstances, nothing else worked against the fear and the feeling that I was engaging with something deeply inhuman. My consultant could never understand why my skin never went red and subsequently gave me the highest dose.

Halfway through one of the treatments, some months later, he came rushing in waving a tiny piece of paper, in obvious distress: the two treatments had overlapped in the middle of my back, and I later concluded that I must have received an overdose of radiotherapy. The consequences were never discussed, far less admitted; later it was as though the incident had never happened. It had taken me all my courage and energy just to go through the procedure let alone think about the consequences and I did not understand until much later what these were.

Six months after the end of the treatment, I began to lose the use of both my legs, the newly gained function of my bladder and bowels and all sensation from the waist down; it went slowly, inexorably, despite physiotherapy, hydrotherapy, curative eurythmy and exercises. I took myself back to the Brook hospital for an assessment; the consensus was that nothing could be proved, it was a combination of scar tissue and nerve damage, they said. I was devastated, I blamed myself, could not understand what it was I was doing wrong when I was trying so hard to get better. I had even managed to start jogging on the cricket pitch near our house, could walk up and downstairs unassisted, was driving again and fulfilling a relatively normal family life. Then it was all taken away again.

'Why, oh why, am I losing the use of my legs?' I asked my doctor, in desperation. There was a terrifying silence that seemed to last forever. I thought… 'He does not know what to say… I have asked him an impossible question.' Then surprisingly he found his answer. 'Maybe you are growing spiritual legs', he said, 'and they may be of far more use to you than my physical legs are to me.' I was stunned, speechless: what did he mean, 'growing spiritual legs?'

That was the start of the spiritual journey I began to take on more consciously in my own life. Spiritual legs must have a function, just like physical ones, but what were they? Bringing the two together took many years of searching for clues, during which time I decided to retrain as a teacher of dyslexic children. The sheer terror of being in a wheelchair was compounded by the fact that I was such a public spectacle when my shyness and self-consciousness had always been such obstacles at the best of times.

Having decided I would start my new training, I engaged myself as a voluntary classroom assistant at a big comprehensive school in Folkestone. I remember driving there in my newly adapted car for the first time, so frightened it almost made me sick. This time I did not need to ask God what to do, I knew already; I said the Lord's Prayer aloud for the last two miles of the journey! Somehow, I got through the doors and started work. My physical pain was still very much there but my experiences at the school proved seminal. I noticed that when I was working my pain subsided; it was quite extraordinary.

I also noticed that my ability to listen to others had become a therapeutic gift, born out of the restrictions my lack of mobility had given to me. Maybe my legs had gone into my ears and my eyes! However, something had not quite clicked, and I was frequently depressed in a rather non-specific region of my psyche. I felt I was not tapping into something essential; I felt very alone and sad. I remember sitting in my wheelchair on a riverbank, looking down into the oily depths of the water one weekend, whilst my husband fixed his boat, thinking that I could just fall in and sink down and down into the water, never emerge again and it would not matter.

Towards the end of my training and one year after my mother had died, I had a keen sense of urgency to visit the clinic where I had been in 1994, as a patient, when still able to walk. It was April 1997, this time something happened that can only be described as a life-changing encounter with one of the doctors of the clinic: the mutual recognition and acknowledgement of a common task seemed to irradiate this encounter with an astonishing degree of intensity. In the silence of the therapeutic space, I remember having the image reflected back to me that, *it was as if some edifice were crumbling.*

From this image an enormous wave of despair cascaded over me. Emergent words sounded from the depths of my soul: 'I want to be well!' In addressing my wellness, despite the disability, my inner life-source felt truly heard, called forth and acknowledged. I felt as though the floodgates to my soul had been opened through the power of these words. In our subsequent conversations, the theme of spirituality came again to the fore; in addressing the spiritual significance of illness, could my disability possibly be seen as a gift? Maybe there are regions of experience that transcend the physical in a tangible way, not abstract, but living realities of inner experience that are like 'other' mountains to climb, valleys to roam and rivers to cross.

Holding this knowledge felt like a very precious gift and gave me the strength I needed to bear my condition; it meant my physical legs had taken me to a place where I could begin another journey that started where the physical one had stopped. For the first time I properly looked down at my legs in the wheelchair, thin, frequently in spasm and utterly useless. I suddenly saw myself as a warrior riding a white horse, my horse was my faithful companion, he was my legs, taking me to places I could not go to on my own. During the course of these adventures and battles his sides had got cut and scraped, he had become old and tired. Nearing our destination at last, he had stopped walking altogether. How I had loved him, I grieved for him, I honoured his faithfulness and now he had taken me to a place where I had to walk alone.

I got up where he had lain down and started walking; I was finding my spiritual legs at last! What this kind of walking meant emerged over the course of the next few years. My will to heal myself, newly awakened, vital, and urgent, became actively engaged with a similar will to put this energy into the service of healing others; it was closely linked with feeling myself upon a spiritual path and having a mission in life that was congruent with my biographical experiences.

Chapter Three
Seven Life and Learning Processes

In acknowledging that birth may not be the beginning nor death the end of life, I experience in this journey that the ego, the self, gathers experience, grows in consciousness, and strives to fulfil its potential. Carl Jung (1875-1961) has described the journey as one of *individuation* in which critical encounters with the external world cause crisis and through these experiences the ego eventually turns inward to discover in polarities, contradictions and shadows a new orientation and meaning in existence. The acknowledgement of a spiritual dimension to human existence extends this notion of the journey considerably.

The transformation and change I experience as a result of finding meaning in the light of reincarnation and karma, has been and still is a healing experience with an illness whose effects are still visible in my own life, in paraplegia, the meaning of which event might otherwise appear to be obscure.

In my study the essence of time is conceived as an organic process of metamorphic development, involving seven stages. Rudolf Steiner named these as the Seven Life Processes[3]. In analysing the stages of my journey and coming to terms with my own illness, I have found this very helpful. The seven stages require experience to be individuated and acted upon.

> *By exploring the spiritual significance of illness, I became someone on an exciting journey of discovery and found purpose, meaning and value in my life's work.*

Transpersonal Experience

My journey leads from physical despair towards a spiritual emergence.

There are many wonders in this world, but none as marvellous as the journey through life itself. This journey is both an outer and an inner one. It flows like a river through the landscape of biography, undulating, meandering and roaming the valleys and mountains of soul experience in an effervescent, sparkling cascade of desire – for what? For that draught, not of forgetfulness, but perhaps of a memory of the things we planned to do and achieve but have not yet done; thoughts that were with us maybe before our earthly life began.

Dreaming our way through this journey is a human condition, familiar to us all, yet how do we wake up within it? Sometimes we awaken in the most difficult of circumstances; we may fall ill, lose our way, and fall by the wayside in despair. We may enter a depression, which at the time does not feel at all like an awakening, but rather an immersion into a thickening mire of unknowingness. It is often at crisis points like this that we admit vulnerability and seek help, or are forced to seek it, despite our conscious intention to the contrary.

We may find that the things we had chosen to do could not be achieved at the time we desired, that life got in our way; that circumstances were not right, that other people's needs had to come before our own. Then there were dams in that river, stones and all manner of obstacles, and sometimes underground tunnels when we could not see the light of day for many miles. Yet still that river flowed on, and like a piece of driftwood we flowed with it, until some inkling of awakening at last occurred. This happening in a person's biography is as unique a moment as the uniqueness of human life itself.

When was the stone so big in that river that we could not swim around it anymore? When did we reach a dam that made us contemplate stillness in the water before the falls engulfed us? When did a hand reach out to us when we thought we were drowning? Did we gaze into someone's eyes who made us remember who we were for the first time? Yet what was it that really awoke in us? Was it the sound of another stream, undercurrent to the river, or even counter-current to the water we thought we knew? Had we met something that made us remember an inkling of our spiritual intentionality in the most unexpected of ways?

A human life is like a river that has a special course of its own. The question is whether we can decipher the hieroglyphs along its course and learn to navigate the river in a way that can inform our conscious passage through it and stop us feeling like a piece of flotsam. Maybe it is initially too threatening to own the meaning of the hieroglyphs since the light of this meaning may be overwhelming. Perhaps we have not yet achieved the necessary psychological maturity to own our power and vulnerability. The most unfortunate of blows in our destiny may sometimes be required to remind us that life cannot continue in the same way, and that transformation and change is needed on our path towards maturity and empowerment.

Reframing and Acceptance

Through encountering a serious illness, I confronted my mortality. It was a painful experience but had an awakening effect on my whole moral relationship to life. Existential change of this nature, especially when guided through therapeutic support, can lead to reframing the conceptual and/or emotional viewpoint in relation to which a crisis is experienced.

Chapter Three: Seven Life and Learning Processes

> *What turns out to be changed as a result of reframing, is the meaning attributed to the situation, and therefore its consequences...*[4].
> Watzlawick, Weakland & Fisch.

Reframing conferred a greater degree of freedom with which to approach my destiny. This facilitated the emergence of wider perspectives in the context of my life. I would submit the thought that one of the greatest gifts one human being can offer another is to be a guide for someone going through such existential changes and so help midwife new meaning in these painful experiences.

As indicated, this has been a cathartic experience in many ways, involving an awakening to the patterns and meaning in my biography. Telling the story is very much part of any counselling process, particularly in bereavement when the client explores the relationship with the deceased, up to the present moment of loss, in order to actualize the loss and come to terms with the grief. In post-traumatic stress disorder (PTSD) contextualizing the trauma in a sequential manner also constitutes a form of storytelling as therapy. Recounting the exact events prior to, during and after the trauma helps to bring rational knowledge and thinking back in relation to psychologically unbearable, undigested emotions. The presence of another (the therapist) can hold the space for and with the client in the 'here and now'.

I looked for common elements which highlight the emergence of the Seven Learning Processes These are derived from the organic, physiological basis as outlined by Steiner in his model of the Seven Life Processes[5] because the organic and psychological processes are so intricately linked.

The Seven Life Processes describe the process of nutrition, i.e. the absorption into the human organism of physical substances.

These metabolic processes can be compared with Seven Learning Processes, as described by Coenraad Van Houten in his work on adult learning processes[6] whereby we take in stimuli through our senses, incorporating these into our existing body of experience and meaning. Since this process also has a physiological counterpart, in that the nervous system is involved, the comparison has a rational basis. In everyday language, we refer to the impact of experiences as needing time to be digested, especially their associated emotions, e.g. in coming to terms with loss. In this case, an experience is digested rather than a meal. Psychology refers to this with the familiar term 'processing'. If part of this activity is skipped or incomplete, it affects the healthy progression to the next stage and a physiological or psychological state of congestion may arise, e.g. an undigested experience may be swallowed down and cause psychological indigestion. To be processed accurately, the experience needs to be recalled, comparable to the need to vomit incompletely digested food. I will chart here both sets of processes to demonstrate their correlations:

Life Processes	Learning Processes
1. Breathing	Observing
2. Warming	Relating
3. Nourishing	Digesting
4. Sorting Out*	Individualising
5. Maintaining	Exercising
6. Growing	Growing capabilities
7. Generating	Creating

*Formerly translated as Secreting, meaning also Absorbing

The first three processes in each list are more concerned with what leads from without inwards; the fourth is the turning point (individualising the food, sense, or experience); and the latter three are concerned with what is directed from within outwards, (what we 'do' with the food, sense, or experience after we have taken it in and how we can eventually be creative with it).

> *Every event of destiny contains a question to which we can find the reply. If we can recognize every event being of the past and a cause of the future, then an open space is created in which the decision is taken as to how we should deal with this present situation.*[7]
>
> Coenraad Van Houten.

This process centers around the notion of transformation, based on 'individualization' at stage four. This is the critical turning point that incorporates the element of struggle as part of the catharsis, from which arises *decision*. It is also comparable to Person Centered notions of developing an internal locus of evaluation, from which to form independent judgements about situations no longer dependent upon external stimuli. The Life and Learning Processes focus not so much on 'knowing', but on 'development as a road to creativity' as a primary principle of engagement.

Analysis through my reflections on the Seven Life and Seven Learning Processes

> *Every one of us can change from merely bearing our destiny to transforming it, and again from transforming our destiny to creating it.*[8]
>
> Ibid.

Life / Learning Process One:
Breathing / Observing
taking in or acknowledging receipt of sensory input.

What did it mean to be growing spiritual legs?

These words were at first incomprehensible to me. All I could do was receive them as a thought. Spiritually speaking, I breathed in this thought, but I could not yet internalise it in a productive way or digest its implications. In fact, I felt overwhelmed by it and put it 'on the back burner'. I was already, on a physical level, taking in my new circumstances as a disabled mother to three young children and this was challenge enough to come to terms with. How would I cope with the cooking, the washing? Would I need help in the house? How would I get down the steps of the house to the drive in a wheelchair? Could I learn to drive an adapted car? These practical questions were paramount at this time; my instinct was about survival.

However, much later, as I reflected on this encounter with my doctor in all its detail, I began to observe both its 'outward happenings and its inward processes'. A third element began to speak to me. It was an invitation to a new thought. This tells us that the outer event combined with the inner experience is expressing something unique about the reality of our own being. The seed of an idea had reached me that I had the possibility to move forwards out of the restriction of my physical immobility in a new way. However, at the time, the thought that spiritual legs might have a practical purpose still lay dormant in me.

Chapter Three: Seven Life and Learning Processes

> *The idea of a journey indicates the notion of movement. 'Classically, the understanding of life, the unfolding of identity and creativity, the notion of growth and discovery were articulated through the metaphor of the journey.'* [9]
>
> John O'Donohue.

We usually have a reason to go on a terrestrial journey, perhaps to visit a new land or explore a different city. Yet mine was something else, it was an inner journey to begin with. Later, it became apparent that I had taken on a commitment to go on a pilgrimage that was more than my inner journey. It was also my commitment to help other people find their own right to journey.

Life / Learning Process Two:
Warming / Relating
(assimilating and adapting oneself to the new information)

I adjusted to the new physical situation over time. After permanently losing the use of both my legs, I learnt to drive an adapted car and retrained as a teacher of dyslexic children, something possible on a one-to-one level. Teaching was something I had originally resisted yet found I loved. I was also struggling with a moral question: should I blame the overdose of radiotherapy for the loss of the use of my legs or should I consider that it had saved my life? Projecting my thoughts ahead, I made a conscious decision to opt for the latter knowing that by adopting the former attitude, a negative environment for myself and my family would be created; this seemed crazy when we were constructively engaged with designing a beautiful extension to the house, fully equipped for my physical needs.

The teaching helped me adjust psychologically too and the training was excellent. I also gained through it a positive sense of purpose outside of my family life. The new work and my positive attitude are congruent with the second Life and Learning Processes, i.e. Warming and Relating. My impulse was to fulfil my part of the 'bargain' with God, who represented the Spirit to me. Like a breath breathed in from outside to inside and then out again, this process appeared in my consciousness spatially. It involved 'warming' towards the situation inwardly. The 'spectator', in stage one, becomes a 'participant' in their own life's script in stage two. The spatial was now linked in my consciousness with the temporal – 'this is me; I am present now and a co-contributor to this situation'.

Life / Learning Process Three:
Nourishing / Digesting
(analysing or breaking down the information into constituent parts to fully penetrate the possible implications of the impact)

> *I noticed that when I was working my pain subsided, it was quite extraordinary… I also noticed that my ability to listen to others had become a therapeutic gift… yet I was still frequently depressed; something had not quite clicked.*

To truly listen, with genuine interest, is a selfless act. The healing I experienced as my pain subsided, struck me in relation to the tremendous potential socially interactive work has as an alternative to painkilling drugs. I began to identify specific and unexpected gifts gained from my crisis, namely the curative effects of empathic listening and my wonder at seeing a synchronicity of events unfold. What previously had appeared to be 'hieroglyphs' began to reveal a new alphabet of understanding. Additionally, by taking these spiritual experiences in creatively, I was being deeply nourished.

> *Digestion transforms the substances we eat into something that can be incorporated into our organism as nourishment and thus made human. The same applies to our psychological learning processes. Our destiny nourishes us only if we digest it properly; if we do not it creates psychological hindrances.*[10] Coenraad Van Houten.

However, despite these insights, my struggle with depression also became a feature of this period and indicated the extent of the inner crisis preceding the catharsis.

The built-in tendency to recover also links depression with the maturational process of the individual's infancy and childhood, a process which leads on to personal maturity, as health.[11]

                                                             Donald Winnicott.

This illustrates a stage of inner development. When the caterpillar enters the chrysalis before it turns into a butterfly, it completely liquefies before the new form emerges.

This image has been used in counselling to describe the potential for transformation that lives in the depressive state. I understood my own depression, in retrospect, to be of this nature. The seed of my own healing was present here in my depressive state. If this were true for me, it could potentially be true for others. However, an inner change needed to come about.

Depression has within itself the germ of recovery.[12] Ibid.

A facilitating environment is necessary for the maturational or recovery process to become active. Maybe this was why, on my own, I felt that something had not quite clicked. The strong sense of urgency led to a desire to revisit the clinic. Did this signify my readiness for emergence from the depressive state, unconsciously sought in a facilitating environment?

Life / Learning Process Four:
Sorting Out / Individuation
(accepting and owning the information and fully assimilating its consequences i.e. changing oneself)

> This is the critical turning point that incorporates the element of struggle as part of the catharsis, from which decision arises. My will to be healed had been met by an equal and equivalent will towards healing.

This fusion generated an inner response that found its expression through my sense of *questing*. My image of the warrior on the horse transformed itself in my mind into the purpose of *spiritual legs*. It meant that I was on a mystery trail in full apparel, despite the fact it had taken me over two years from hearing about the spiritual legs to discovering their use.

By consciously experiencing the depression, I felt liberated from its grip. This enabled my pre-pupa state in my chrysalis to receive its new form; I felt 'knighted', worthy of my suffering, and courageous. I had found meaning through an *'aesthetic experience of tragedy'*[13] and was inwardly enlivened by this experience. A sense of catharsis pervaded me. The encounter enabled me to reflect and gaze beyond what I had previously perceived in the first three stages. This was something to do with my destiny as a future task, as I was only too aware, given the power of the meeting that had engaged my thoughts, feelings and actions in a transformational way.

Action

Finding out what that task was leads me into the next cycle of research, here I describe the emergence of the workshops. This new departure signified the Fourth Life and Learning Processes now becoming active within my psyche. The process of transformation I experienced now became individuated, meaning that I separated out the essential message from the non-essential. It became for me a living question:

> *How might I put my experiential knowledge into a form that was both helpful to myself as a creative project and helpful to others experiencing similar crises?*

There arose two principal developments. The first was an article in which I wrote about my experiences with a view to inviting others on a similar journey of discovery. The article described the full history of the coming into being of the workshops, how the impulse was born from a period of reflection on this critical life event, in collaboration with colleagues. It was publicly communicated in the form of an article, to which people were invited to respond.

The article contained four principal points:
Receiving support.
The inner journey or road of discovery.
Deciphering the alphabet / finding meaning.
Recognising others on the journey, mutual help.

The second development was the coming into being of the workshops called 'Building Bridges', to which those who heard the invitation came. The workshops were inspired by the principles of the Seven Life and Learning Processes. These principles took shape in creating the possibility for others to be guided into these Processes, as I had myself.

Life / Learning Process One ~ Breathing / Observing:
Helping others to learn about spiritual legs and inviting them on a journey of discovery.

Life / Learning Process Two ~ Warming / Relating:
Adaptation to the new situation, empathic listening to each other's stories and developing coping strategies.

Life / Learning Process Three ~ Nourishing / Digesting:
Reading the signs for creative potential within us and attempting to incorporate them in our lives, building confidence.

Life / Learning Process Four ~ Sorting Out / Individuation:
Enabling potentially life-enhancing encounters to arise through working in groups with biography exercises, research questions and artistic activities – developing meaning.

In the year following our stay at Park Attwood Clinic in 1997, my friend Valerie and I stayed in close touch. A letter written to staff at the clinic was followed by a preparatory retreat with some former, interested patients, therapists and doctors in May 1998. The date for the first workshop for patients was then scheduled for May 1999.

Year by year we added themes to our workshops, such as 'the inner and outer journey', 'encounter', 'thresholds', 'the spiritual significance of illness', 'healing – the individual and the community', sometimes having one per year, others two or three, travelling to many different parts of the country and eventually to Ireland. Participants came from all over the country; some recovering from serious illnesses, some with unresolved medical conditions, others seeking a way out of depression or trying to find meaning in other kinds of life-crises such as redundancy, bereavement, or divorce. Many people felt they were deeply affirmed in their personal journeys and went on to lead more fulfilling and creative lives. Others came back for further workshops as a boost to their own development and a sense of continuity with fellow travellers. It was a rare thing if people left disappointed; we always gave space for feedback on the last morning and encouraged constructive criticism as well as positive comments.

In 2002, the clinic, which had provided the space for Building Bridges inception, hit a crisis more profound than any in its twenty-one-year history. That same year I separated from my husband of twenty-eight years, and my relationship to Building Bridges changed. I no longer felt able to carry the work forward primarily on my own and put out a call to extend the carrying group membership. In November 2002, I also put in a funding proposal to a sympathetic charity and was successful in obtaining a substantial sum, which yet again confirmed and validated the work. However, the transition was not easy and a carrying group retreat in 2003 confirmed that I was still necessary in the steering seat.

There was an eighteen-month pause in our work followed by more workshops, all of which have been slightly different in character to the previous ten. The first of these addressed more specifically a conscious decision to embark on a path of self-development with the theme 'invitation to the inner journey'.

In October 2005, a request came from the Patients & Friends of Anthroposophic Medicine (PAFAM). This was our first 'task' oriented group, i.e. a group already working together regularly and seeking ways to understand their task in the world more fully. They wished to develop a better understanding of group dynamics to serve the association's needs. As a committee member of this association, I was requested to be a participant and not a facilitator for the first time on any of my own workshops. I saw this as a tremendous compliment to the validity of the work of Building Bridges and a personal success in enabling the 'child' to come into its own as an adult and not be dependent on me as the 'mother'. I was excited to see my fellow carrying group members managing well without me and I could relax in my new role as a participant.

Another new request was designed as a festival workshop and given back as a gift to the clinic, in which Building Bridges had found its inception. The theme was 'Christmas as the Festival of Wisdom and Love' (December 2005). This was a unique event in many ways.

There also came a 'child' of the Building Bridges initiative, called Oasis. This project is currently situated in different places, now both in this country and abroad, and runs three pathways of twelve weeks each. Each Oasis pathway corresponds consecutively to each of the three days of a Building Bridges Workshop, developing more slowly and fully the considerations of biographical development. 'Remembering' for the first pathway, (*Spirit Recollection*); 'self-management' and 'self-management strategies' for the second pathway, (*Spirit Awareness*); 'confidence building and finding our creativity' for the third pathway, (*Spirit Beholding*). It draws its ethos from the Foundation Stone Meditation given by Rudolf Steiner in 1923 to the members of the Anthroposophical Society.

Life / Learning Process Five:
Maintaining / Exercising
a systematic repetition of all preceding processes
until they become habitual.

> *Year by year we added themes to our workshops… Many people felt they were deeply affirmed in their personal journeys and went on to lead more fulfilling and creative lives.*

However, on many occasions, I was inwardly in agony. I had said 'yes' to a process of change, within myself, that required an almost unbelievable degree of courage, especially because I was, in many ways, still timid, shy, and not self-confident. The courage I had needed to exercise earlier on, in relation to going under the radiotherapy machine and driving to school to teach, was called upon repeatedly in initiating the workshops and carrying responsibility for them. I would lie on the bed shaking and in a cold sweat for several hours before giving a talk at a workshop. Yet miraculously, once I was in the social space, calmness came over me and no one ever knew the agony I had gone through. I began to recognise this pattern and accept the resistance and its trials, which did get better with time and practice.

Exercising can be likened to 'practising' which means coming to grips with resistances. In meeting these resistances, we develop capacities that appear as new capabilities in the next learning step, 'growing'. However, the dynamic process interacting between 'individuating', 'exercising' and 'growing' needs to be continually practiced. I consider the 'practise' of running different workshops contributed to my own learning of what worked and what did not work in diverse groups of participants. Through this activity, I grew new capacities and skills as a facilitator, learning about my own strengths and weaknesses in the process. The following two stages will be summarised, as I believe the reader has now gained an insight into the research process and can begin to explore and cognitively elaborate the methodology themselves, in relation to my narrative.

Life / Learning Process Six:
Growing: new capabilities
extending one's scope and possibilities for effective action through the foregoing, effecting change into the world.

> *There have been many more workshops...*

Out of the learning received from the previous step I developed more self-confidence to embark on new ways of meeting my own creative needs and interest in trying different types of workshops and similarly, positively responding to the tangentially new requests that were coming towards Building Bridges. I was finding an *'ability to act freely and creatively in the destiny situations life presents us with.'*[14]

Life / Learning Process Seven:
Reproducing, generating
the changes of Six assume independent life in the outer world.

Enabling the child to come into its own as an adult and no longer be dependent on the parent.

Generating can be seen in what emerges from the original impulse and becomes independent as it reaches another level of maturity. It becomes fertile as a progenitor of new growth and generative, as in the Oasis Project and the initiatives of the Oasis Trainings finding independence.

A Pilgrimage

As part of my research process, I sought the opinion of others, to develop my peripheral vision, raise consciousness, question my assumptions, and identify my own standpoint. To this end I talked to several colleagues who had gone on personal pilgrimages by foot and on horseback. I found my inner journey had similar thresholds to theirs but were differently experienced. They were interested in my process and methodology and were unanimously moved by my story and the workshops that had arisen from it.

However, during supervision for my thesis it became obvious that the wide scope of my research made it difficult to bring the different qualitative elements together and I had to re-start my dissertation from the beginning, just at the point when I had provisionally completed it. This was a difficult experience; the potential for using the results in my professional work were exciting.

My research process entered a *pralaya*. A depressive mood overtook me and other life events pertaining to my family and my health also enforced this rest. However, on reflection this period proved to be a valuable time of gestation, of gathering new insights and developing a personal maturity which had not previously been available to me. I focused more specifically on my own story as the point of departure for recommencing the new dissertation. This then provided the required personal container for the piece to unfold in.

'*He that be a pilgrim*', declared the London preacher Richard Alkerton in 1406, '*oweth, first to pay his debts, next to set his house in governance, and afterwards to array himself and take leave of his neighbours, and so go forth*'.[15] Identification with our context is crucial to taking up the invitation to the journey. From this step a 'dis-identification' can occur which brings about a freer relationship to certain attachments and personality structures, or 'sub-personalities', which we need to recognise to move forward.

Pilgrimage is not only about 'what' we meet but 'how' we meet it. We meet 'time' in the experience of our biography through the events that befall us. We meet 'space' in our innermost being as we internalise these events as processes of transformation. It has become much more difficult in our high-speed, modern age to consciously engage in these processes. It is precisely this that inspires people to go on old pilgrim routes by foot to experience time and space differently along with the catharsis that travelling brings.

> *Traditionally a journey was a rhythm of three forces: time, self, and space. Now the digital virus has truncated time and space. Marooned on each instant, we have forfeited the practice of patience, the emergence and delight in the Eros of discovery.*[16]
>
> John O'Donohue.

I found the discovery of the inner journey an exciting process. The sense of adventure is great, the trials terrible and the rewards delightful. I identified twelve rites of passage in *The Hero's Journey* which the traveller may also have to navigate:

1) Invitation / Call.
2) Meeting Resistance.
3) Finding Helpers.
4) Being Given the Instrument of Power.
5) Threshold.
6) Meeting the Guardian.
7) Confrontation.
8) Resolution.
9) Supreme Ordeal.

10) Reward.
11) Threshold Back Again.
12) Return Home.[17]

Many of these stages correspond to the ones I heard about in my conversations with modern day pilgrims and the responses these called up as they encountered inner trials of doubt, fear, grief, loss, and acute feelings of homelessness, so to develop the courage needed to continue their path. More pertinently I hear their resonance in the journey through an illness. In the recognition of inner disharmony, a self-knowledge is called up that leads to something like an awakening of the will to find healing.

A colleague who undertook a pilgrimage a few years ago, suggested to me that a little bit of healing must happen first to wake up to the possibility of a journey and to the taking of initiative… There is a mystery in finding the right pace and when you have found it you must honour it, because it connects you to the earth in a way that increases your knowledge of what you owe to it for your existence. Not only are you connecting to your own will, but you are connecting to the will of the earth, in effect to your destiny with it.

We are born into a social context as human beings, part of a family or tribe, a culture, and a society. We have an individual identity within this and our interaction with others enables us to fulfil our creative potential, whether we are artists, musicians, scientists, parents, politicians, road sweepers or criminals. We become more fully operative when we can engage with our fellow human beings. Our freedom to engage in this drama of life is dependent upon many factors, our social and cultural context, our sociological conditioning, our personality, our health and most importantly our self-knowledge.

In finding an 'inner compass' with which to orientate myself,

I realised that developing interest in and caring for other people, their lives, their suffering, their trials, and achievements, was essential to finding my own meaning, purpose, and value. I had taken on a commitment to go on a pilgrimage in the company of others.

> *My commitment was to help other people find their own right to journey.*

This identification of a goal or destination to my own pilgrimage was resonant with the ideology that lay behind the therapeutic endeavour of Park Attwood Clinic, where I had first found healing and meaning. Their premise was that there was a spiritual significance to illness and that the potential for health could be found through anthroposophical medicine and therapy in a community setting. It was through a combination of these factors that I was inspired to co-found the Building Bridges workshops and subsequently the Oasis Project with groups in other places too, primarily through looking at the *spiritual significance of illness*.

The idea was that inner nourishment and healing could begin to take place outside the clinic in these workshops. People could thereby meet, engage in meaningful encounters, and bring their own experiences and spiritual research questions together supported by artistic activities and lectures. Thus, could seminal experiences gained in Park Attwood flower from the same tree in other places, nurturing the patients and supporting the spirit of the clinic at the same time. Through an encounter we experience another person; they experience us and through this exchange we begin to know ourselves.

> *It seems clear that when we are seen, understood and respected, our sense of being expands as the riches of human development unfold… in effect, the empathy of the other allows us to develop self-empathy.*[18]

The value of group work in this respect is indisputable for the management of health issues, including the potential to support longevity. It can be particularly helpful for cancer patients. Developing an understanding of the Life and Learning Processes, particularly in relation to the way we manage illness, has engaged me throughout this research. Our senses act as portals through which we meet the outer world and our environment. As we internalise and process this information in our personality and psyche, it subsequently contributes to our developing maturity.

Through our biographical relationship to the environment (nature), we internalise these experiences (nurture) and finally own them at the deepest level of our being (individuation). On the assumption that spirit exists in higher forms of self-awareness, the symbiosis of outer and inner, as it meets the self, or ego, thereby reveals itself as the pathway to finding the spiritual imprint of the human being within the physical organism. If humanity is to become aware of its spiritual origin and destination, which as I believe is one of the most important pathways to health, we need an understanding of the body as temple of the spirit. My personal philosophy defines developing maturity in terms of an accompanying spiritual and psychological self-awareness.

Reviewing one's biography out of an acknowledgement that we are body, soul and spirit can assist us in this process. Thus, the inner and outer journey come together in our life experience, through the Seven Life and Seven Learning Processes. As we take hold of these life processes physiologically then through the activity of our ego or self, the accompanying learning processes can follow.

> *This learning is also about the recognition that we have a spiritual human being within us who is the wise guide to our destiny calling.*

Chapter Four
The Spiritual Archetype of the Journey

What would my life have been like without this journey?

In considering the significance of this question, I should explain that shortly after the critical turning point in my late thirties, I had been lying in bed and unable to move. Yet movement is the key feature of travelling and setting out on a path. I had found that in looking at the way the wind moved the branches and leaves of the tree outside my window, I could become one with their movement too. It seemed like flying, exhilarating and a little scary, like having a flying dream and not quite knowing where you were going to land; however, I had been wide awake.

While exploring these feelings, I had also learnt to drive again in an adapted car, one fitted with hand controls. The experience of managing roundabouts had been disorientating. My sense of movement was no longer grounded through my legs, as previously experienced. Yet the lack of physical movement in my legs gave me the feeling that my journey was being guided by forces within myself that were invisible to me. This led me to observe how people generally walk. I noticed that the act of walking is, for the most part, taking place at an unconscious level. To raise walking into consciousness requires an act of will and a keen awareness of our inner motivation.

The more I reflected on this, I began to wonder whether this new insight might help to compensate for not being able to use my physical legs any longer. This resonated with what my doctor had said earlier, namely that I might be growing spiritual legs. Those spiritual legs might have a tangible purpose after all. I began to realise that we walk through our will, our inner motivation towards something, although we are asleep to this reality most of the time.

I surmised that I must therefore learn a new method of orientation. It was like learning to read a new language with a completely different alphabet, yet my everyday reality at that time had been travelling between Canterbury and Maidstone, a sharp contrast.

I also experienced unusual interactions with other people. Once, when I was rolling at speed down Canterbury High Street over the cobblestones in my wheelchair, I hit a larger cobblestone than anticipated and I fell out right in front of the careening wheelchair. Miraculously I was not hurt. Two strangers walking past just picked me up off the ground, one on each side, as if they were used to this kind of occurrence. They put me back on the wheelchair, briefly enquiring if I was alright and then walked off in different directions. Astonished by the ease and speed with which this had happened and the help that had become available, I carried on to my destination.

On another occasion I was attending a training session on dyslexia. I had a big pile of books on my knees. It started raining hard and I was struggling to keep the books steady while steering the sliding wheelchair on the wet tarmac. Suddenly, a pair of hands grabbed the handles of my wheelchair and started pushing it rapidly up the hill to the doorway I intended to enter. At the door, a young man's voice said, 'Don't worry, there will always be one of us here to help you,' and then he vanished in the pouring rain to another building, a mindful student perhaps?

Once, I was late for a meeting, but my intention and energy were such that I entered the outer doorway to the community room at such speed that the interior door swung open, seemingly of its own accord and I avoided entanglement with handles, hinges, locks and wheels. I arrived exactly on time.

> *These impressions all gave me the sense that I was back on track with my purpose in life and that help would unexpectedly appear so long as my motivation was clearly informing my direction of travel.*

It was at this point that I began to meet other inner thresholds, for example by confronting the source of my depression. Life before my disability had not exactly been easy, but neither had it been without its joys. However, pre-existing feelings of self-doubt and despair were now magnified in the face of the loss of the use of my legs, often leaving me feeling completely powerless. At such times I would find support and comfort by listening to Bach, where possible in art galleries sitting in front of old masters' paintings such as by Giotto or Cimabue or reading certain texts by Rudolf Steiner.

At times my disorientation was such that I felt myself to be deep underground in a dark cave with the thundering sound of waves all about me. At others, I found myself in a kind of joyful expansion into sunlight that was impossible to sustain. During this critical time, I sometimes swung between these polarities like a pendulum, as if caught in a dynamic.

In sharing these experiences with certain friends, my attention was drawn to Steiner's lectures on the Hibernian Mysteries. Hearing how others, albeit in former times, had needed to encounter similar experiences in the path of their own development overcame my sense of isolation. I felt seen and newly grounded. It was as if I were being reaffirmed in my connection to the universally human and reconnected to a shared human experience. My metaphorical feet had landed on the path. The inner and outer journey had begun, coherent, present and exciting. I felt full of life and wellbeing. The way ahead now became far more comprehensible, manageable, and meaningful.

The idea of a journey is one that expresses adventure and the promise of unexpected things to come. For me, these elements come together in the following tale, a remarkable narrative, which includes the spiritual, mostly unseen field in which we all participate. It takes the form of a spiritual diary covering seven days. I shall tell this tale in my own words. It is derived from *A Christian Rosenkreutz Anthology*[19]. I first encountered this tale in a drama workshop in which I participated during 2002. To this day my experience remains vibrant, appearing like a portal or stepping-stone on my life path.

A Significant Tale

My own paraphrase of *The Chymical Wedding of Christian Rosenkreutz*

On the first day in this story, we find a wise old man living on the side of a mountain in a hut. He is eighty-one years old and has travelled through many continents, seeking to share his wisdom with others and gain new insights. He is a very humble person and lives life simply and in harmony with nature. He has learnt the secrets of healing, both of body and of soul. In his later years, he assumed his travelling days were over, so he sought to deepen his understanding of the simple things encountered each day, the rocks, plants and animals, the springs and rivers, the changing seasons with their storms, clouds and sunshine. These are all a source of constant wonder and mystery to him. He loves the scented bright flowers, visited by butterflies and likens these to small airborne flowers, dancing in the sun.

Sometimes he meets other travellers on the mountainside who seek his company and his healing herbs. He helps each one as best he can. His life is simple yet rich and full. When storms rage, and threaten to overwhelm his little hut, he laughs in joy at the sheer exuberance of life. Sometimes it seems that the roof of the hut will be blown away. Yet it remains well secured, and when the sun returns, he is thankful.

For some time now a feeling had been growing in his heart that he must go on another journey. He experiences such moments, full of movement, like the joy of a song on the wing. Stronger and stronger this feeling grows and when least expecting it, these were unexpected moments, sometimes just before dusk, when the earth rejoices with the day's gifts and heaven's night has not yet begun, or when watching the skylarks soaring in flight or listening to the call of birds. His heart beats faster at thought of this journey.

Easter is fast approaching, the year he turns eighty-one. One day, as he is eating the simplest of meals, there is a tremendous rushing of wind that threatens to tear the open window from its hinges. Is it a freak storm perhaps? Yet he can see no cloud on the horizon. Sensing that something or someone had blown in through the open window behind him, the hair on his neck rises. Too terrified to turn around, he feels a tap on his shoulder, which gives him an almighty start. He feels another tap. Whoever or whatever it is has not gone away and eventually he turns around and sees a shining being dressed in blue robes covered in stars with glorious wings all colours of the rainbow, covered in eyes, standing there.

Under her arm is a bundle of letters. Picking a small letter out of the stack, she puts it carefully on the table. Then, blowing a golden trumpet with a mighty blast of sound, she vanishes as swiftly as she had seemingly arrived. For a full fifteen minutes afterwards, his ears continue to ring. Astonished, he looks at the envelope. It appears to be glowing with light. Tentatively, he reaches out his hand to pick it up, and very nearly drops it again because it feels as if it were made of solid gold. He eventually opens the envelope and realises the letter inside is an invitation. Experience tells him that moments like this need time to be properly digested and he thinks that if by some chance the letter is real, it will still be there in the morning. He then retires to bed.

That night he has a dream. In the dream, he finds himself held captive in a tall, round tower; one with no windows and only a small trapdoor at the very top, high above him. All around him there are many people lamenting and crying to be let out and fighting one another for a foothold on the rocks which rise in places from the floor of the tower. Occasionally the trapdoor opens, and a rope is let down.

Whoever is nearest to the end of the rope clings on for dear life and is hoisted out by an ancient man and woman on top of the tower.

When the trapdoor opens once more, our traveller has scrambled onto a higher rock close to the inside of the tower wall. By some chance the rope swings across to him. He grabs hold of it and is hoisted out. Once at the top he receives a gracious welcome from the ancient man and woman and is told that as he has been so blessed to escape the tower, he must shortly go on a journey. Finding he has sustained a knock on the side of his head from the wall, he sees some drops of blood have splashed onto his tunic; he also notices he has sprained his foot.

On the second day, when he awakens from his dream in the morning, he feels refreshed and realises that the dream had some meaning. He notices, oddly, that his foot still aches. Picking up the letter still lying on the table, which seems far lighter this morning, he sees it is indeed an invitation – to go to a wedding.

He is filled with a sense of relief and confirmation at the sight of this visible proof. This is the journey he has been waiting for, and now as an invited guest. He puts on his best white tunic and a handsome straw hat into which he threads four red roses. About his chest he crosses a braid of red fabric. From his belt, he hangs a water bottle and a bag into which he puts some salt and bread as sustenance for the journey. Leaving the hut, he starts walking through the forest. The birds sing and the wind blows lightly through the leaves on the trees, making them dance and glitter in the sun. He feels as light and buoyant as a youth and whistles a little song to the birds as he strolls along.

Once out of the forest he comes to a crossroads on the path by some tall trees. To one of the trees is fastened a notice which says that whoever wishes to continue to the wedding must now choose one of four ways. One way is steep and rocky and quite dangerous but faster, one is long and circuitous where you might easily lose your way; one way is only for those of royal blood, and one is a fiery path not suitable for mortals. Unsure which way to go, he settles down under a tree to consider the matter and take some refreshment.

As he is eating his bread, a little white dove flies down and he amuses himself by feeding it some crumbs. Suddenly a black raven swoops down to chase the little dove away to get the bread for itself. He jumps up to follow the dove and finds he has left his bread and the bag behind under the tree. Attempting to turn back is quite impossible because a mighty wind is blowing so hard, he can barely breathe. Yet if he continues forward the way becomes manageable. He realises he is now on one of the four pathways, although we are not told which one it is: the way has been chosen for him without his conscious choice in the matter.

That night he arrives at a castle and must pass a terrible lion on the way that roars in a frightening fashion until it has been calmed by its guardian. Choosing to spend the night in the castle hall with some other humble travellers, he nevertheless notices that other guests are being led to the royal bedrooms.

The following day, the third, he is courteously shown some of the wonders of the castle by a gracious Virgin named Alchemia. He is also shown a large globe of the universe. All the many guests who are gathered there are being weighed on a great pair of scales to ascertain their readiness to participate in the wedding. Our traveller's weight is surprisingly great. He is subsequently able to share this surplus weight with another guest who weighs too lightly. Some guests weigh very little indeed and it pains him when they are then thrown out of the castle. We are led to understand that weight, in the sense of this story, is not a physical attribute.

Chapter Four: The Spiritual Archetype of the Journey

On the fourth day, the remaining guests are taken to a great hall where six Kings and Queens are seated. Surprisingly, the guests have been summoned to witness the Kings' and Queens' beheading. Yet from this seeming death comes forth new life, as is later revealed.

On the fifth day, the guests, our traveller included, are taken by ship across a lake to an island. Here in a tall tower, seven storeys high, they are instructed in the making of healing medicines from plants and minerals. At each of the seven levels, different processes can take place for restoring the beheaded royal persons to life.

On the sixth day, at the sixth storey in the tower, a snow-white egg emerges from the medicines heated in a golden globe. An unusual bird hatches from the egg and is cared for by the guests. After many transformational processes take place, two tiny figures are moulded from a special dough and given the life-giving medicines. These two tiny royal people are destined to become the next King and Queen. They quickly and miraculously grow into maturity whilst sleeping, as if in a dream, along with the assistance of the guests and our traveller, whose help is needed for them to begin to breathe in their new life. This process happens under the guidance of the Virgin with utmost sacredness.

Our traveller witnesses a streak of spiritual fire that shoots down into the sleeping King and Queen from above the roof of the tower that awakens them. The reborn King and Queen now awake in wonder and joy from their deeply transformative sleep and descend through all the seven levels to the foot of the tower and then quietly return by ship to the castle, to prepare for the next day.

On the seventh day, all the guests who have laboured in preparation for the alchemical wedding, along with the Virgins, return over the lake in many sailing ships to the castle. It is the reborn King and

Queen's wedding, to which our guests and many others have been invited. At the very end of this spiritual journey, our traveller thinks he has not been able to fulfil his tasks adequately in preparing for the wedding. He is half-jokingly told that because of his doubt he must therefore remain the doorkeeper until someone else can replace him. In truth he is the one guest best prepared. However, he takes this news seriously enough and it devastates him. He believes he must accept this fate.

The wedding then takes place. All the guests experience a glorious inner awakening at the sight of the alchemical wedding and find their rightful homecoming in their own ways, including our worthy traveller who can now return to his home ... *here several pages are missing from the tale* ... our traveller awakens in his hut.

* * * * * * *

Whilst you must read the whole tale to learn about the many mysteries our traveller sees in the castle and the wedding itself, this tale uses images to reveal processes of transformation and change. It speaks of how one way of consciousness is continually transforming into another through our own inner striving.[20]

What I wish to portray and draw attention to is the impact this tale made upon me. We are being invited to let go of old ideas and form quite new thoughts in response, just as if we were participating in this unusual, puzzling and surprising journey ourselves. Several pages appear to be missing at the end of this ancient book. Their whereabouts remains a mystery to this day, just like the liminal[21] spaces in our own lives, where what is in store for us is not always known. A deeper awakening is invited by our determination to travel and is achieved through our endurance and good courage for personal truth. When joy emerges on this path, it is as if by grace.

I have been intrigued by this tale for many years and my fascination remains to this day. The tale is full of imagination, richly colourful, deeply human and soulful. The inner and outer journey is one to which I can personally relate. Certainly, such journeys do not often come together quite so poignantly as in this tale. However, I believe that if we look deeper into our own lives, many mysteries can be revealed and be seen to unfold as if in a richly coloured tableau. The traveller appears to me today like an inner witness who signals that we are given the choice and opportunity to consciously embrace the essence of the spiritual that lies within us, alongside our journey towards personal individuation.

I find it awe inspiring how the seven days of this story describe a spiritual journey that can emerge from and affirm the Seven Life and Learning Processes. I have already highlighted in Chapters Two and Three that when life processes unfold physiologically and transform into learning processes psychologically, they link together and bear witness to an awakening of the spiritual journey which accompanies them.

I share below seven contemplations which arose from my initial participation in the drama workshop on the Alchemical Wedding. They are like shining seeds buried deep in the soil of my biography, waiting to grow into the light and be seen. The contemplations can also be understood as notes for a future study. In their essence they reveal the whole drama of my life and of this book.

Seven stages of a journey's archetype

These stages can be seen as time organs relating to an individual's biography. They may also represent the journey of an individual in relation to an organisation or community to which they are connected. Based on the Seven Life and Learning Processes, they give a physiological basis to understanding the archetype of the inner journey of the soul in biographical development. They are also given an imaginative expression in the imprint of the alchemical journey of Christian Rosenkreutz.

The Rosicrucian aspect of this path implies that each stage in one's life takes on the quality of a rite of passage or sacrament. In attempting to draw these threads together, I had the opportunity to speak to three contemporary pilgrims who made journeys on foot or on horseback, to Santiago de Compostella and the Karlstein Castle; these are traditional pilgrim routes. I then linked my findings with some of the inner thresholds I met on my own personal journey. I have given the name Pilgrimage (d) to this part of my study as it encompassed the terrestrial and biographical aspects as well as the soul and spiritual journey.

Each of the seven contemplations indicate the connections I found between:

a) The Life and Learning Processes

b) The day of the Alchemical Wedding

c) The Rosicrucian path as a rite of passage

d) A Pilgrimage.

First stage

a) Life Process: Breathing ~ Learning Process: Observing
b) The Alchemical Wedding, First Day: The Invitation
c) Rosicrucian Rite of Passage: Study
d) Pilgrimage: Preparation.
Take in the message and become motivated.

The decision to go on a pilgrimage when walking on foot is both a conscious decision and a preparation for the start of the journey. As a life crisis or illness experience, it is an unconscious preparation and invitation to embark on the inner journey of self-discovery. Finding a functional balance between that which is circumstantially given through the environment, and social and family structures in one's biography, forms the basis of our striving for individual expression and creativity.

Second stage

a) Life Process: Warming ~ Learning Process: Relating

b) Alchemical Wedding, Second Day: Choosing a way and arrival in the castle

c) Rosicrucian Rite of Passage: Imagination

d) Pilgrimage: Right Rhythm.
Adapt one's former self to the new direction.

Our will is engaged in the activity of walking, through which we must find a 'right rhythm'. An operative, if not perfect balance is needed for walking. Movement is expressed outwardly and physically through walking and in self-directed activity. Adapting oneself to the new direction helps to free us from old restrictions and one-sidedness. We begin to see the path of life differently. New signposts are revealed, pointing us in the right direction. To read these signposts imaginatively may be called developing a sense for seeing the universal within the personal.

> *The image of the black raven, which snatches the food offered to the white dove evokes in the soul of the traveller a certain feeling; and this feeling, produced out of supra-sensory, imaginative perceptions, leads along the way that ordinary consciousness would not have been permitted to choose.*[22]   Rudolf Steiner.

Third stage

a) Life Process: Nourishing ~ Learning Process: Digesting

b) Alchemical Wedding, Third Day: Weighing

c) Rosicrucian Rite of Passage: Reading the occult script

d) Pilgrimage: Going barefoot, courage, loneliness.
Carefully assess one's own obstacles and those which life presents and attempt to see them as belonging together.

Going barefoot, either literally or figuratively, means we reconnect our will to the will of the earth. We make ourselves receptive to our environment in a different way and to the working of our own inner life of soul, wherein we may have felt frozen. Courage is needed to walk in this new way, to face the sense of loneliness that comes from the separation we must experience from familiar surroundings and the habits of daily life. We explore an inner landscape that is necessarily different from that which we knew before. This means that we also become more vulnerable in awakening to these changes. Withstanding the tension between what we were before and our new way of being, increases our resilience, just like exercising a muscle increases its strength.

Taking in these new experiences liberates our conceptual life, which becomes inner nourishment, explicitly seen in the life and learning processes. In the alchemical wedding, the weighing of the travellers ascertains their moral preparedness for learning through life experiences. Do they have sufficient self-knowledge and the resources to continue to the next stage and are they conscious of where they fall short and where they are strong?

The sign for something physically and spiritually meeting can be indicated by two intertwining spirals, the one leading inwards and the other leading outwards, not quite touching in the middle.

Fourth stage

- a) **Life Process: Separating out, discerning, discriminating ~ Learning Process: Individualising**
- b) **Alchemical Wedding, Fourth Day: Beheading**
- c) **Rosicrucian rite of passage: Preparing the philosopher's stone**
- d) **Pilgrimage: Vulnerability, determining one's own threshold, encounter, responsibility.**
  Submit oneself with complete commitment to one's goal and follow one's own inner judgement as to what this entails to the bitter end, e.g. discerning the essential from the nonessential. Meet the unknown with commitment. Powerlessness meets empowerment.

This stage is a crucial one. The vulnerability we have allowed ourselves to experience has been gained through hard inner work and by developing an open attitude to the new circumstances we find ourselves in. This puts us in the position of being able to determine our own thresholds, i.e. What is right for me to experience now is a new determination that must be constantly reassessed. This is the threshold where the wheat and chaff get sorted. By way of example, the pilgrim I interviewed who went on horseback, took the challenge to cross a hazardous bridge despite her vertigo. She shut her eyes and bravely held onto her horse's tail in front of her, whilst walking. Finding she gained much strength from taking on this challenge in the unusual way she did, found she was later able to tackle an even greater obstacle, open-eyed and with much more confidence.

The right rhythm established earlier, in the ability to walk freely into new possibilities and transformation of the self, can now be turned

Chapter Four: The Spiritual Archetype of the Journey

into creating a right rhythm in our breathing. This eventually leads to a metamorphosis of death substances into life-giving substances. The possibility of renewal is already here. In the mineral world, we can see the transformation of coal into diamond, both lower and higher manifestations of carbon. In the plant world, we know that the plants breathe in carbon dioxide and breathe out oxygen. Human beings and animals alike need oxygen to live, whilst we breathe out carbon dioxide.

The Rosicrucian rite of passage, preparing the philosopher's stone, is a symbol of the transformation of this breathing process in the human being into life giving forces. See the mystery of red and blue blood in the human heart, as it listens and responds to our life's activity.

Rosicrucians work in the real world, right down into human physiology. They work at transforming the earth and the human being, not merely on the level of moral improvement, ennobling behaviour and so on, but right down into the physical body.[23]

Rudolf Steiner.

Fifth stage

- a) Life Process: Maintaining ~ Learning Process: Exercising
- b) Alchemical Wedding, Fifth Day: Making medicines
- c) Rosicrucian rite of passage: Knowledge of the microcosm, our essential human nature
- d) Pilgrimage: Maintaining the dialogue and faithfulness.
  Find the motivation to continue in the wider context of life, putting the impulse into ongoing practice, developing patience.

This stage is to do with knowledge of the self, how can we hope to remain faithful to our journey if we do not find a creative dialogue between ourselves and our environment. As we penetrate the peculiarities of human nature and reflect upon our own life of soul then intensify this study with knowledge of our physical being, right down into its physiological construction and constitution, our bones, organs, blood and nerves, we come to a greater perception of how we relate as a microcosm to the bigger macrocosm, to the cosmos as a whole.

The power to recognise the great, universal self is attained through immersion in the organs.[24]

                                                    Rudolf Steiner.

Sixth stage

    a) Life Process: Growing ~ Learning Process: Growing capabilities

    b) Alchemical Wedding, Sixth Day: The Egg (all seven within it)

    c) Rosicrucian rite of passage: Becoming one with the macrocosm.

    d) Pilgrimage: Recognition of others.
Witness new faculties, skills and patterns emerging and own the newly arising power in a selfless way as the power to heal.

The macrocosm now speaks to us personally and universally, through having gained knowledge of ourselves as a microcosmic picture of this universe. Everything gained can now be put into free relationships, to meet others openly, to experience the world meaningfully and be engaged in how it speaks to us. As we begin to do this, our own skills become world skills, our own life becomes of service to others and the world. We recognise the 'other' as having something essentially to do with us. True encounter is possible in a balanced way where self and other begin to dialogue and create the power to heal, self, other and world.

Seventh stage

- a) Life Process: Generating ~ Learning Process: Creating
- b) Alchemical Wedding, Seventh Day: Homecoming
- c) Rosicrucian rite of passage: Beatitude
- d) Pilgrimage: Arrival, homecoming, healing.
  Allow the results of the journey to reveal their new message and await further moral intuition.[25]

The arrival is not easy; it is won through endurance of the most difficult trials and self-doubt. There is in this stage, the ascension of our higher self out of our lower self, which leads to a blissful feeling of oneness with all life and being. The sevenfold human being is symbolized by the cross wreathed in seven roses.

Knowledge now becomes feeling, what lives in the soul is transformed into spiritual perception. We begin to experience ourselves in all beings; a stone, a plant, an animal, and everything in which we immerse ourselves. They reveal to us their essential nature, not as words or concepts but in our innermost feelings.[26]

Rudolf Steiner.

Further reflections on Building Bridges and the Oasis Project ~ the catalysts

The enrichment I have experienced through hearing about the spiritual journey in an imaginative form, alongside the physical and soul stages of development and individuation, has uniquely impacted my life and awakened and inspired my creative sensibilities, whether this was through working with groups of people or in my painting. The name given to the Second Pathway of Oasis is *Finding a Way* and expresses for me our search for personal individuation. It appears to me like a metaphor for a life lived, loved, and learned. Initially the Building Bridges workshops, which preceded Oasis, were designed as weekend events starting on a Friday afternoon and continuing until Sunday lunchtime. On the Friday afternoon there were introductions to one another and to the weekend. As preparation for the workshop, participants were asked to bring a life question relating to the leading topic or theme, for example, the Spiritual Significance of Illness or the Inner and Outer Journey. The life questions were broadly grouped together then shared individually in smaller groups on the Saturday morning. During the afternoon everyone engaged in artistic activities, such as painting or clay modelling or walking in nature.

The evening was for relaxing and breathing out with storytelling, singing and music. On the Sunday the whole group gathered and shared what they had gained from the workshop. Many insights sprang from these reflections in the group setting, contributing to individuals finding a more meaningful way forward in their lives and work. Some experienced this as a transformational step.

Each of the three days invited us to bring something from our past experiences, something about the present circumstances and something as a resolve for the future. Broadly speaking, these themes were also given spiritual value, that of *spirit recollection, spirit mindfulness* and *spirit beholding*. The aim of the Building Bridges Workshops was therefore one of community building, which included shared meals, personal stories, and artistic activities. Its form came through first hearing about the Upper Room Meetings and the meaning behind the Camphill communities[27] in conversations with Valerie Wright in 1997.

The Oasis Group Project, on the other hand, aimed to bring these three broad themes into weekly meetings for participants who sought to reclaim meaning in their lives. The meetings were held over the period of three terms. Like Building Bridges, Oasis had also been deeply inspired by the spiritual substance of anthroposophy, as profoundly expressed in the Foundation Stone Meditation[28] and aimed to link our biographical, developmental, and spiritual being together into one awareness. These groups were specifically meant to compliment anthroposophic medical-therapeutic work and focused more on soul development. In a creative collaboration of artistic work and self-reflective or biographical exercises, a new resource was provided for people who were perhaps living with unresolved health conditions or suffering loss and anxiety or disillusionment. Three consecutive Pathways provided the structure for self-refection, self-exploration and personal growth and offered opportunities to access hidden sources of creativity, resilience, and well-being latent within each of us.

Chapter Four: The Spiritual Archetype of the Journey

Names and themes of the three Pathways of Oasis, indicating their rites of passage:

Pathway One: *The Inner and Outer Journey*

Pathway Two: *Finding a Way*

Pathway Three: Embracing the Challenge.

You can hear how these themes correlated with those from the tale of the Alchemical Wedding and show how deeply the tale resonated with me throughout each of these projects. A further fourth Pathway remains open like the missing pages from the traveller's tale; its gesture is one of liminality, another threshold between one way of being and another. It would be my wish for this fourth Pathway to be interpreted by the different group members in their own unique ways; living creations arising from participating in the previous three pathways.

I remain intrigued about the choices we make in our lives; the things we cannot change and the things we can make conscious decisions about. There are also those choices which we do not immediately understand but are influenced by our participation in the whole complex field of life.

Summary

Oasis aims to address the whole human being in body, soul, and spirit. The following points illustrate this intention:

- To help to provide a wider appreciation of health and well-being, rather than focusing on illness.
- To address each person's hidden potential and facilitate an active engagement with their healing process.
- To offer a safe environment where people may share and speak out freely about experiences and support one another.
- To provide biographical and artistic exercises to encourage greater understanding for the patterns and paths in life.
- To explore sources of inner and outer creativity.
- To awaken hope, love, and new purpose in life by mastering the emotional life rather than being swamped by it.
- To acknowledge that there is an inner journey that runs parallel to the outer one.

Conclusion

I offer this closing thought on liminality as being a critical part of any journey, process, or pilgrimage. It includes three main elements, the experience of separation, that of liminality and that of integration. However imperfect we may feel ourselves to be, we are all artists in life through our creative engagement with it. We then take on purpose and meaning by imprinting our own unique contribution on to life's rich tapestry. I experience that writing this book and drawing the threads of my life together has also been the integration of a journey.

As an artist myself, I enjoy sensing space through the interplay of light and form to where the liminal places lie. These transitional spaces inspire and hold a source of wonder and mystery for me. Through looking out into nature in the interplay between fluid, air and light I find movement and inspiration for my painting.

This book has been about my life from a threefold exploration, an alchemy of body, soul and spirit, whose literary expression comes into being through the metaphor of the journey. In it I wished to convey how certain themes have developed in my own life, myself as microcosm within the greater macrocosm.

I would like to give thanks to all those who have made this journey possible; through their nurture, nature and through their friendship and participation; and particularly to my three children, Laura, Edward, and Rob who have given me so much joy and love throughout my life and to my grandchildren.

Melanie Taylor, August 2023.

References

1. Rudolf Steiner, *The Riddle of Humanity*, GA 170, Lecture 15th August 1916: The Sense-Organs and Aesthetic Experience. Rudolf Steiner Press 1990.
2. William Hutchinson Murray, *The Scottish Himalayan Expedition*, J. M. Dent and Co. 1951.
3. Rudolf Steiner, *The Riddle of Humanity*, GA 170, Lecture 12th August 1916: Twelve Senses and Seven Life-Processes.
4. Watzlawick, Weakland & Fisch. *Change. Principles of Problem Formation and Problem Resolution*, Norton, New York 1974, p.95.
5. Rudolf Steiner, *The Riddle of Humanity*, GA 170, Lecture 3rd September 1916, Rudolf Steiner Press., London 1990.
6. Coenraad Van Houten, *Practicing Destiny*, Temple Lodge, London 2000.
7. Ibid.
8. Ibid.
9. John O'Donohue, *Divine Beauty. The Invisible Embrace*, Transworld, London 2001.
10. Coenraad Van Houten, *Practicing Destiny*, Temple Lodge, London 2000.
11. Donald Winnicott, *Home is where we start from*, Penguin, London 1986, p.72.
12. Ibid.
13. Rudolf Steiner, *The Riddle of Humanity*, GA 170, Lecture 15th August 1916.
14. Coenraad Van Houten, *Practicing Destiny*, Temple Lodge 2000, p.123.
15. Jonathon Sumption, *Pilgrimage: An Image of Mediaeval Religion*, Faber & Faber, London 1975, p.168.
16. John O'Donohue, *Divine Beauty. The Invisible Embrace*, Transworld, London 2001, p.27.

References

17. Joseph Campbell, *The Hero with a Thousand Faces*, Pantheon Books, USA 1949.
18. John Firman and Ann Gila, *The Primal Wound*, SUNY, New York 1997, p.80.
19. Paul M. Allen and Carlo Pietzner, *A Christian Rosenkreutz Anthology*, Rudolf Steiner Publications, New York 1981, p.67.
20. See Dennis Klocek, *The Alchemical Wedding. Christian Rosenkreutz, the Initiate of Misunderstanding*, Lindisfarne Books, New York 2001, and Rudolf Steiner, *The Secret Stream*, Anthroposophic Press, Great Barrington, USA 2000.
21. The word liminal comes from the Latin word 'limen', which means threshold. A liminal space is a place of transition, a time of waiting and not knowing the future. Richard Rohr describes this space as: '...where we are betwixt and between the familiar and the completely unknown. There alone our old world is left behind, while we are not yet sure of the new existence. That's a good space where genuine newness can begin.' Richard Rohr, *Everything Belongs: The Gift of Contemplative Prayer*, The Crossroad Publishing Company 1999.
22. Rudolf Steiner, *The Secret Stream*, Anthroposophic Press, Great Barrington, USA 2000, p.168.
23. Ibid, p.91.
24. Ibid, p.57.
25. Verbal communications referring to, d) Pilgrimage, given in a workshop on 'The Seven Life Processes manifesting as Living Processes of Soul Development' with Dr James Dyson MD, Park Attwood Clinic, 2002.
26. Rudolf Steiner, *The Secret Stream*, Anthroposophic Press, Great Barrington, USA 2000, p.58.
27. Karl Konig 1902-1966.
28. Sergei O. Prokofieff, *Rudolf Steiner and The Founding of the New Mysteries*, Temple Lodge, London 1986, pp. 347-9.

Bibliography

M. Abu Talib & W. West W. (1998) *Hearing what research participants are really saying, the influence of researcher cultural identity.* Counselling and Psychotherapy Research, volume 2, No 4, 2002.

Paul M. Allen & C. Pietzner, *A Christian Rosenkreutz Anthology.* New York. Rudolf Steiner Publications, New York 1981.

A. Antonovsky, *Unravelling the Mystery of Health.* Jossey-Bass Inc. 1987.

R. Assagioli, *The Act of Will*, Platts, Woking 1974.

J. Benson, *Working More Creatively with Groups*, Routledge, Oxon 1987.

P. Broadhurst & M. Hamish, *The Sun and The Serpent*, Pendragon Press, Cornwall 1989.

P. Broadhurst & M. Hamish, *The Dance of the Dragon.* Cornwall. Mythos, Cornwall 2003.

British Association of Counselling & Psychotherapy, *Code of Ethics & Practice.* Rugby 1998, 2005.

J. Bowlby, *Attachment and Loss.* Volumes 2 and 3, Pimlico, London 1998.

Bruner, *Actual Minds, possible worlds*, Harvard University Press, USA 1985.

J. Campbell, *The Hero with a Thousand Faces*, Pantheon Books, USA 1949.

I. Clarke, *Spirituality and Psychotherapy*, PCCS Books, Ross-on-Wye.

P. Clarkson, *The Therapeutic Relationship.* Whurr, London 1995.

Padraic Colum, *Myths of the World*, Floris Books, Edinburgh 2002.

James Dyson, *Soul-Size*, Portal Books, Hudson, NY 2022.

R. Elliott, C. Fischer & D. Rennie, *Evolving guidelines for publication of qualitative research studies in psychology and related fields.* British Journal of Clinical Psychology volume 378, 1999.

P. Ferrucci, *What We May Be*, Tarcher Penguin, New York 1982.

V. Frankl, *Man's Search for Meaning*, Rider, London 1959.

Bibliography

A. Frank, *The Standpoint of the Storyteller. Qualitative Health Research* volume 10, May 2000: pp354-365

D. Freshwater & Rolf, *Critical Reflexivity: a politically and ethically engaged method in nursing*, N.T. Research 6 (1). 2001.

Firman and Gila, *The Primal Wound*, SUNY, New York 1997.

I. Gordon-Brown & B. Somers, *Transpersonal Psychotherapy. Innovative Therapy in Britain* 1973.

S. Grof, *Spiritual Emergency*, Tarcher/Putnam, New York 1989.

J. Heron & P. Reason, *A Short Guide to Cooperative Inquiry*. Holistic Health Volume 68, Spring 2001

W. Hutchinson Murray, *The Scottish Himalayan Expedition*, J. M. Dent and Co. 1951.

Karin Jarman, *Touching the Horizon*, Temple Lodge, Forest Row 2008.

Dennis Klocek, *The Alchemical Wedding. Christian Rosenkreutz, the Initiate of Misunderstanding*, Lindisfarne Books, New York 2001.

E. Kubler Ross, *On Death and Dying*, Routledge, London 1970.

M. Jacobs, *Psychodynamic Counselling in Action*, Sage, London 1998.

C. Jung, *The Archetypes and the Collective Unconscious*, Princetown University Press, USA 1969.

J. Lees, *Reflexive Action Research: developing knowledge through practice*. Counselling and Psychotherapy Research. BACP Journal, 2001.

A. Linley & S. Joseph, "Post Traumatic Growth." *Counselling and Psychotherapy Journal* volume 13 (1). 2002.

A. Maslow, *Towards a Psychology of Being*, Princetown University Press, USA 1962.

J. McLeod, *Doing Counselling Research*, Sage, London 1994.

C. Moustakas, *Heuristic Research*, Sage, London 1990.

Murray Parkes, *Bereavement. Studies of Grief in Adult life*, Penguin, London 1996.

M. O'Brien & G. Houston, *Integrative Therapy. A Practitioner's Guide*, Sage, London 2000.

J. O'Donohue, *Divine Beauty. The Invisible Embrace*, Transworld, London 2001.

D. Ornish, *Love and Survival*, Vermilion, London 1998.

D. Polkinghorne, *Narrative configuration in qualitative analysis*. J. Amos & R. Wisniewski (Eds.) *Life History and Narrative*. Routledge Falmer, Oxon 1995.

Sergei Prokofieff, *Rudolf Steiner and The Founding of the New Mysteries*, Temple Lodge, Forest Row 1986.

C. Rogers, *A Therapist's View of Psychotherapy*. London. Constable and Company, London 1967.

R. Rohr, *Everything Belongs: The Gift of Contemplative Prayer*. The Crossroad Publishing Company 1999.

H. Salman, *The Social World as Mystery Centre*, Threefold Publishing, USA 1999.

Virginia Sease & Manfred Schmit-Brabant, *Paths of the Christian Mysteries*, Temple Lodge, Forest Row 2003.

Peter Selg, *Karl Konig: My Task*, Floris Books, Edinburgh 2008.

Schumacher, *A Guide for the Perplexed*, Harper and Row, New York 1977.

V. Sinason, *Attachment, Trauma and Multiplicity*. East Sussex. Brunner Routledge, East Sussex 2000.

Rudolf Steiner, *Anthroposophy (A Fragment)*, Anthroposophic Press, New York 1970.

Rudolf Steiner, *Mystery Knowledge and Mystery Centres*, Rudolf Steiner Press, Forest Row 2013.

Rudolf Steiner, *The Secret Stream*, Anthroposophic Press, Great Barrington 2000.

Rudolf Steiner, *The Riddle of Humanity*, Rudolf Steiner Press. London 1916.

J. Sumption, *Pilgrimage: An Image of Mediaeval Religion*, Faber & Faber, London 1975.

Bibliography

M. Taylor, *The Archetype of the Journey in Relation to Giving Meaning to a Serious Illness or Crisis*. MSc Dissertation, University of Greenwich, London 2006.

C. Van Houten, *Practicing Destiny*, Temple Lodge, Forest Row.

Watzlawick, Weakland and Fisch, *Change. Principles of Problem Formation and Problem Resolution*, Norton, New York 1974.

W. West, *Psychotherapy and Spirituality*, Sage, London 2000.

A. Williams, *Fairies and Enchanters*, Nelson & Sons, New York 1943.

Winnicott, *Home is where we start from*, Penguin, London 1986.

Worden, *Grief Counselling and Grief Therapy*, Tavistock, New York 1983.

Isabel Wyatt, *From Round Table to Grail Castle*, The Lanthorn Press, Cornwall 2005.

H. Zimmerman, *Speaking, Listening, Hearing*, Lindisfarne, New York 1996.

Zulueta, *Attachment, Trauma and Multiplicity*, Brunner Routledge, East Sussex 2002.

About the Author

Born in 1955, Melanie Taylor attended Wynstones School, a Steiner Waldorf School in Gloucestershire, being fortunate in having Rudi Lissau as a teacher. After leaving school, she completed a BA (Hons) at Canterbury College of Art in 1977 and went on to marry and have a family. After a severe illness left her permanently disabled in 1993, she retrained, initially as a teacher, gaining a postgraduate diploma in Professional Studies in Education at the Dyslexia Institute in Kent in 1998 and later as a therapeutic counsellor, receiving an MSc in Integrative Therapeutic Counselling from the University of Greenwich in 2006. She additionally audited the Foundation Year and first year of Training in Psychosynthesis Psychotherapy at the Institute of Psychosynthesis, London, between 2004 and 2006 and found this study deeply affirmative.

Between 2004 and 2016, Melanie was invited to become a faculty member and presenter on a CPD Seminar for Mental Health, an anthroposophical training sponsored by the Medical Section at the Goetheanum, designed to meet the needs of mental health workers, social therapists, and therapeutic educators, subsequently held at Emerson College, Sussex.

Melanie went on to develop her own original programmes in adult group work, especially designed for those in search of spiritual meaning in their lives, many of whom were also living with chronic illness. These interactive groups, inspired by her studies and enriched by her understanding of Rudolf Steiner's descriptions of the Seven Life Processes, also included storytelling and creative artwork. In 2010 and 2012 respectively, she founded and directed *Oasis Group Facilitation*, two training programmes designed to promote succession. She was a co-founder and executive director of the Elysia Therapy Centre in Stourbridge from 2012 to 2021.

Melanie has three children and eight grandchildren and enjoys painting, writing and being a grandmother. She is a member of the Anthroposophical Society, of the Christian Community, and of the Camphill Community. This study, spanning the course of her life and portrayed as a spiritual and psychological journey, underpins *The Sevenfold Journey*. The genre is autoethnography.

This is her first book.

Wynstones Press
publishes and distributes a range of
Books, Advent Calendars, Cards and Prints.
For further information please see:

www.wynstonespress.com
info@wynstonespress.com